MW01601590

THE OCCULT NATURE OF GOD

QUESTIONING THE NATURE OF DIVINITY

TARL WARWICK 2016

COPYRIGHT AND DISCLAIMER

INTRODUCTION

Within this text, an attempt has been made to arrange the existence of a creative or divine force or being into eight distinct groupings- limiting them on three factors- whether this is a deity or intelligent being, whether or not there is a form of eternal or significant punishment for disobeying it, and whether free will exists in a literal sense or is either absent or illusory in nature.

The purpose of this text is not to disprove that a deity exists although I myself do not practice any organized religion, but rather evaluate the possible characteristics of a creative or divine force using this system.

Throughout the centuries mankind has worshiped a vast array of beings and forces- from the purely creative to the mixed, and from (subjectively speaking) pure good to pure evil- these beings are discounted within this text, as presupposed, self evident entities, and subjected to logical examination from a system in which eight distinct possibilities exist- ranging from an all benevolent creator, to a tyrant deity, to a cosmic force possessed of creative potential without actually being possessed of its own goals or volition.

There are, truly, many ways to classify the existence of a divine being, multiple such beings, or a creative cosmic force- one could probably choose from thousands of characteristics and philosophical ideas behind religious forces and arrange many such charts and possibilities.

THE OCCULT NATURE OF GOLD

I have chosen free will and punishment for the primarily reason that both of these facets feature heavily within most organized religions- purely that, within most religions, it is widely accepted that there is *some* organized manner by which human beings are judged either worthy or unworthy by a being or force and subjected to a punishment or reward thereof (usually post mortem) and it is widely accepted that, essentially, *this system operates properly because humans are possessed of a true, and literal, capability to obey or disobey divine command, and thus are themselves both subject to judgment, and capable of rendering the verdict thereof through their own actions and thoughts.*

This philosophical writing attempts to remain unbiased- merely pointing out the eight possibilities of divinity according to this system, and rendering unto these eight possible outcomes judgment from both a scriptural (or religious) angle, as well as a more humanistic, emotional angle which, while purely emotional and possibly fallacious, is nonetheless a major basis upon which reality is experienced by most human beings.

Within this work the word "god" or "deity" refers to an intelligent, motivated, force or being, with some sort of goals, known or unknown, which creates physicality and administers, if present, punishment or judgment, and which is presumed to be exceptionally powerful, if not all powerful, in nature. This being is differentiated from a "cosmic force" or nonexistence of an entity primarily by the presence of intellect or personal volition, an arbitrary but useful definition that coincides with the nature of a deity as described by most organized religion.

Examples of systems which are exempt, logically, from these eight categories, will also be discussed.

POSSIBILITY ONE: THE SELF LIMITING DEITY

1. There is a deity or deities

2. This deity or deities makes use of punishment for rule breaking.

3. Free will exists.

The first possibility of divinity is, of course, the one which is stressed mainly by proponents of organized religion- in short, that there is some sort of (normally all knowing and all powerful) creator figure at the center of existence, and that this being has, variously, given us scriptures within which are contained rules and laws for humans to follow- either within a culture or religion.

This being is further described as making use of punishment for infractions of these laws or rules, often eternal punishment, or else temporary but grueling punishment, for things which people have transgressed.

Within this system, typically, man is considered to have a *choice* to follow these laws or not- for their very ability to obtain salvation, or divine favor, depends upon their ability to choose their course of action.

As we investigate such a being, we are naturally led

to a startling conclusion- this supposedly all-powerful, all-knowing, eternal, irrefutable, illustrious being is, in fact, not actually all knowing and, thus, cannot by definition be omnipotent either (for complete power requires complete knowledge.)

If we assume that mankind has free will, is it truly possible for the being to know mans' actions beforehand, without becoming a tyrant which casts people into Hell knowing beforehand (and thus being the determiner of their actions rather than them) that they would fall into sin?

The inability of this deity to actually be all knowing is best summed up with a simple paradox involving an apple and an orange.

You have, before you, upon a table, an apple, and an orange. You are now free to pick either one. Let us say this all knowing creator figure *knows* you will choose the apple. (This is a simplified situation, but works within the context of disproving omniscience in relation to free will.)

Since this being has determined beforehand that the apple will chosen- the dilemma is as follows: *are you capable of ignoring the apple and choosing the orange?*

If you are not able to choose the orange, because the being has already determined the apple will be chosen, free will is by definition an illusion, and the result of a limited mentality on mans' part.

If you are free to choose the orange instead, you

have by definition proven god wrong, and invalidated its own completed omniscience.

There are those within the spiritual community who thus claim that this being does not know your *specific* choice and outcome, but merely all *possible* outcomes, but this is an error on their part- knowing the possible outcomes is not a form of omniscience, unless you also know the specific outcome.

It seems logical that within this system, it is not actually possible for a deity of an omniscient nature to coexist with free will.

In short, the first possibility of divinity, is merely that there is a deity (or multiple deities) which punish for infractions in accordance with true, honest free will on the part of man... and the conclusion here is that this being, or these beings, or this force, cannot actually be all knowing- literally that gods are limited in power, as were the ancient pagan gods, a threefold conclusion that is ironically supported by most Christians and Muslims and Jews, while actually showing that their notion of an all knowing deity is not possible.

This, interestingly, would invalidate the widely held beliefs of most large religions, almost all of which claim their deity is all knowing, while also claiming as a basic tenet of faith, that man must be free to choose punishment or salvation- acknowledging that otherwise the being(s) would be tyrannical in nature and unfit to be worshiped.

POSSIBILITY TWO: THE TYRANT

1. There is a deity or deities.

2. This deity or deities makes use of punishment.

3. Free will does not exist or is an illusion only.

The second possibility of divinity, is as follows:

A deity exists, this deity makes use of eternal or temporal punishment for infractions of law or rules, and free will does not exist.

Within this system, infractions of the law or of rules, or of whatever moral structure favored by this deity, are punished, but man does not have free will, and thus the capability to remedy his situation, being predestined for either some sort of salvation, or some sort of hellfire, through no capacity of his own.

Such a being should be viewed objectively at first in an unbiased nature, for there are no logical problems within this classification whatsoever- merely that this being, on a more subjective scale, would be infinitely tyrannical, and that most of mankind would likely shun such a being for worship, passing it over as just another evil force to be ignored, avoided, or refuted as devilish.

However there are those who worship such a being-the Lutherans famously disavow the existence of free will and do indeed believe in a fated, predestined existence within which only some people are actually saved by their deity to live in eternal bliss, and such groups seem to spread primarily by making use of a slightly modified appeal to flattery, indicating that by joining such a group, you are part of that special chosen group that is fated to enjoy your eternal existence.

More to the point: such a deity could indeed exist, for it is not my goal here to disprove that a deity is real or false, but merely the conclusive natures of such a proposed deity should free will and punishment be used as limiting features.

Such a being would be best classified, in an unbiased sense, as a being concerned mainly with rules, rather than people themselves, a being for whom which organization of components is more important than the components themselves, and one which is primarily concerned with its own plan rather than those existing within it.

It could be that such a being considers life ultimately unimportant- which does in a tangential way make some sense, as such a powerful being would by necessity view all life forms as relatively small and powerless by comparison.

Summing up this being in a more humanistic sense, it would be a being more closely resembling "evil" (as far as the term is appropriate) idols or demons, rapacious beings with an insatiable appetite for war or sacrifice, than the being proposed by most large religions.

Indeed, the existence of such a being would negate the nature of most groups within modern theism, and most humans could hardly believe such a creator could exist given the subjectively "beautiful" and functionally useful world around them.

It could however be that polytheism is reality- in which case one could envision a rather benevolent, Zeus-like creator that nonetheless has appointed some other divine creature to administer death and punishment who, like Hades, possesses many morbid, pain-obsessed traits and operates autonomously from the creator deity.

POSSIBILITY THREE: THE BENEVOLENT BOHEMIAN

1. There is a deity or deities.

2. No punishment exists.

3. Free will exists.

Perhaps the most "nice" of possibilities, is the infinitely benevolent being which reigns over existence, with mankind free to choose his own adventures and actions, but where that being or beings do not administer any sort of structural punishment for rule breaking, with all punishment either being temporary and limited, or not existing in any form at all.

Such a being does not seem to coincide with most large religions- although there are groups that stress that because of some cosmic circumstance or temporal individual, punishment either no longer exists (has been nullified by another force) or is strictly temporary- the more liberal groups within Christianity variously believe in a sort of purgatory for infractions of a completely temporary nature (after which all individuals enjoy eternal bliss) or that there isn't even this temporary purging, and that upon death all individuals of necessity will enjoy eternity together in happiness.

Within this possibility, unlike the next, free will also exists- although it is unclear whether this free will extends to the proposed afterlife or reincarnation cycle, with of course, Tibetan Buddhists claiming the reincarnated individual will choose his parents before reincarnating, and some fringe groups claiming paradise to be a place without physical restriction, in which the departed and reinstated are free to fly around, eat what they want, enjoy carnal pleasure, or anything else they may wish, for eternity.

Such a being does, however, cast serious doubt on the larger corpus of organized religions, most of which claim that there must be some sort of separating the "wheat from the chaff" so to speak- that because the creator god, or pantheon, is infinitely good, there must be some sort of purging process before the wicked enter paradise, or else that there is no purging process and that, thus, the wicked will be eternally incapable of entering bliss.

This bohemian existence seems rather utopian-mankind is uninhibited by predestination, and suffers no specific set of punishments for actions regardless of whether they violate the laws and morals laid down by any organized religion.

This could be summed up as the negation of organized religion itself- that is, that while a deity exists, it hasn't been adequately explained by any supposedly holy text, and that organized groups espousing a deity similar to this possibility, have come to the right conclusion by using the wrong names and scriptures, for a casual review of most holy books precludes a deity that does not punish its subjects for infractions.

POSSIBILITY FOUR: THE DETERMINISTIC AUTOMATON

1. A deity or deities exist.

2. No punishment exists.

3. There is no free will.

A second benevolent being, perhaps best summed up as the deist's creator- a being which does not punish mankind for wrongdoing, either because this being is logical and orderly, and understands it would itself be subjectively evil should it punish beings which it did not give free will, or else because the being itself, creating humans in its own image, thus created them in a mechanical manner rather than a truly unique, personal one.

Some groups have suggested such a cosmic force-including theistic determinists, who insist that a creative force (usually intelligent) has indeed structured the universe but that, due to an infinite regression, all outcomes and actions were predestined.

Perhaps in order to distance themselves from the concept of good and evil (which itself would be in question in an infinitely regressive system) these individuals often declare that as the creator deity is infinitely good, that no form of significant punishment could exist for breaking moral rules, purely because this would verge into tyranny.

There is a logical problem here- the determinist theist has applied human logic to a cosmic problem, which may operate outside of physical, observable logical systems- indeed such a being would be rather mechanical to our eyes, perhaps viewing mankind as toys, or perhaps being an actually unintelligent force, a machine of sorts, in turn created by another even more potent being (which in itself becomes another infinite regression.)

However such a being as suggested is not a tyrant-no punishment exists in this system, even though true freedom to determine ones' actions is equally false. Rather, this might be imagined as a bizarre sort of infinite system in which regression reigns and the universe operates in a very mechanized fashion, operating upon a completely linear continuum, with only the illusion of choice.

This invalidates most religions on both fronts- on the first, because many of them, as I have before stated, include the concept of punishment from a divine source, in regards to breaking holy law, and secondly, because most religious groups consider free will of importance in their cosmology.

In fact, to my knowledge, there is not a single large religious group that believes in such a mechanical deity, which is neither malevolent nor benevolent, but merely exists in some preconceived fashion, with existence itself another machine manipulated or built by this being or force.

POSSIBILITY FIVE: THE COSMIC JUDGE

1. There is no intelligent deity or deities

2. Punishment for wrongdoing exists.

3. Free will exists.

The fifth possibility of divinity- that there is no truly autonomous, intelligent force at the center of existence but that, somehow, there is both a system of punishment in place for breaking laws, morals, or rules, and that humans possess the free will to either follow such rules, or disobey them and be punished.

Such a force at first seems impossible- for without an intelligence behind the rule system, how could punishment for breaking these rules actually exist?

On further exploration, we can see that, just as a plant may dispatch chemicals to kill an attacking, foraging animal, so too could a non-cognate force or life form structure existence by its own unintelligent, random hand, creating order through some unknown process without itself being actually possessed of intelligence.

Such a force can exist- it need not be an intelligent; for existence could have come about through completely random chance, guided by a cosmic existence which nonetheless does not possess mentality.

It could be easily believed, that through no specifically intelligent reasoning, punishment exists merely as an offshoot of random chance- that reality merely "happened to structure itself in this manner." However, as before, this belief would negate the likelihood of many religions, not merely because it posits the creative force to be unintelligent, but because of the strictly random or unordered nature in which punishment and free will coexist.

This belief is prevalent among certain less defined, semi-theistic new age groups- they posit that a force created existence, and is orderly in nature, but rather than ascribe this force an anthropic characteristic (gender, intellectual capacity, true goals or motivations) they ascribe it with a sort of purified existence- that it is literally extant, but is merely a manifestation of order itself, as opposed to chaos, which some such groups imagine exists in realms outside its own ordering effect- that without this system there is pure chaos.

The flip-side of course to this non-inspirational but real system of order, is an equal force, dichotomous to it, but roughly outside of the concept of dichotomy, as envisioned by certain groups practicing chaos magic, a force which has been described personally to me as a sort of anti-cosmic soup in which progenitor beings (often identified with the figure of Lilith) created "bubbles of experience" within the chaos, existing solely to experience existence itself both within and without chaos- until the aforementioned dichotomously opposed demiurge or lower deity, broke away from this and created order in another realm, which they imagine as a degenerate idea.

POSSIBILITY SIX: THE ORDERED MECHANISM

1. There is no intelligent deity.

2. Punishment exists.

3. Free will does not exist.

The sixth possibility is that there is no deity, but

rather a cosmic force or order/pattern through which punishment exists, but in the absence of free will. This somewhat mentally challenging possibility can logically exist- perhaps order merely exists simply because *order must exist* for whatever philosophical reason- and if such a force does exist, it must be pure order for orders' sake and also mechanical in nature, for without free will, it could merely be a function of existence itself, that for a primordial reason punishment, objectively seen, has less to do with the individual and more to do with circumstance, much as with a machine made by mankind, a part may melt or break down not due to its own congenital defect but due to chance.

However, this is a force that seems not to have been posited by a religious group- for while the Lutherans cast aside the notion of free will and embrace the idea of punishment, they include an intelligent being in the mix, and the new age groups which cast aside an intelligent deity may include punishment (or not) but almost invariably believe humans through some method are able to alter whether or not punishment applies to them.

In any case, the mere casting aside of such a force being intelligent in nature would invalidate most scripture, because scriptural morals are, more often than not, based upon the notion that an intelligent force had a hand in crafting the guidelines by which order and usually punishment is administered to the human species.

This orderly mechanism is somewhat paradoxical in nature- if it is not intelligent but there is still a form of divine punishment, any believers in such a force are tasked with explaining the basis upon which such punishment is meted out, as well as of course its actual nature, something which would be perhaps possible, but not for certain.

It does however release itself from the paradox of possibility five, in that there is no need to explain how free will objectively and literally exists if there was no intelligence behind it but while such a force still resulted in the presence of a divine form of punishment for those breaking rules- either written or unwritten, which it manifested.

POSSIBILITY SEVEN: NON DETERMINIST ATHEISM

1. There is no deity.

2. There is no punishment for wrongdoing.

3. Free will exists.

Within the seventh possibility is included the realm of atheism- in short, that there is no deity of an intelligent nature, that creation may be guided by some cosmic force or may be the result of pure mathematical chance, and that there is no defined system of judgment or punishment (and by definition in this particular system, that man creates moral structure and that there is no objective, divinely inspired definition of right and wrong.)

THE OCCULT NATURE OF GOLD

In this particular case- free will exists, thus mankind, unburdened either by punishment or objective law is essentially free to operate at will, doing whatever he wants- it is a common belief within atheism, that this is the case, and believed by hundreds of millions (perhaps billions) of people.

There is however here also a paradox- for free will, volition, capability of choice, within such a system, seems in itself difficult to fathom- many atheists within this grouping have explained this as such- that *free will, while possibly illusory in true nature, nonetheless functions because the mentality of a human being is not all knowing.*

There is also the possibility of an unintelligent cosmic force at play in creation with this possibility- but nonetheless one which neither designs punishment nor operates in a mechanical fashion- some new age movements posit this- that humans may do whatever they wish without fear of punishment, guided only by order as created by the confusing hand of some force as yet unexplained by mankind.

In this existentialist state, we do not necessarily discount that there is a continuation of consciousness post mortem, but rather that regardless of its existence (as reincarnation or as an afterlife) its function would be based upon some as-yet unexplained scientific phenomenon (quantum theory touches on this very vaguely and in a non-theistic manner as well) rather than based upon the equally as-yet unevidenced assumption that a deity influences the process.

THE OCCULT NATURE OF GOLD

Some cope with this paradox by designing that the purpose of their existence in such a system is purely biological- a sort of church of science that boils existence and all matters down to living for the sake of reproducing and maintaining a physical form, while other groups cope with it by proclaiming that, while there may be a purpose beyond mere physicality, this purpose is either unexplainable, poorly explained but alluded to, or else purposely hidden from mankind, as with some groups that believe in a form of enlightenment without judgment behind it.

This system may also be used by those who believe human life was engineered by a different, formerly more potent and wise life form, as the Sumerians suggested with the Annunaki, or as modern pseudoscience suggests is the case with alien life forms they themselves attempt to describe- whether this is deterministic and regressive in nature is purely split into two opposed groups, with the deterministic form described under possibility eight.

The Sumerians further seem to explain this dichotomy in a perhaps psychologically relevant manner, with the being Enki observing mankind at first possessed of no free will, but introducing them to it by means of either genetic engineering or of a possibly hallucinogenic substance which increases their mental capacity, freeing them from the slavery of Eden, identified therein as a sort of work camp rather than paradise.

POSSIBILITY EIGHT: DETERMINISTIC ATHEISM

1. There is no deity.

2. There is no punishment.

3. Free will does not exist.

The atheistic determinists are separated from their non determinist counterparts in essence, solely by their refutation of free will, and their adoption of a non-infinite universe or existence, which at some point was created, as the atheistic groups believe, by either scientific phenomena or random chance, purely that if existence and consciousness did not exist, *we would not know it because we would not exist.*

From the deterministic point of view, existence is arranged into a repetitive, infinite regression, in which one progenitor action at a point in time many eons ago, created existence (without an intelligence behind it, normally) and that because of physical laws, with each atom and subatomic particle moving in a specific direction at a specific speed, with all of its attributes accounted for and if not actually known, at least possible to know, that all events past present and future, are predestined, and that free will is illusory.

One could imagine that if infinite regression was

true, that if you had a machine capable of calculating the movement, energy, and state of all particles within existence at the same time, you could not only see every moment of the past by running your calculations backwards, but also see the future by running them forwards, even observing yourself observing yourself-another paradoxical statement.

This possibility is believed by determinist atheists-those who deny the existence of a deity (sometimes on the basis of this same regression) and ascribe existence and creation to an unknown force of science (usually physics) which may or may not be described as the big bang.

Unlike the non deterministic atheists, they would likely not agree with the oscillating or multiverse models-precisely because a universe which oscillates infinitely would disprove an infinite regression, while a true multiverse model taken to its logical extent, would invalidate the idea of a truly closed or limited system, and thus render some physical laws nonexistent.

In such a system, morality itself is in severe turpitude- and the only point of existence could possibly be to exist, because without the notion of free will, it would not make sense, say, to punish those who break secular laws, because they were fated to do so in the first place, through no intelligent volition of any higher power.

It is not clear that even an unintelligent cosmic force could exist within such a cold mechanical system either, as such a force would itself have been created, again as with former possibilities, leading to an additional infinite regression, hearkening to the somewhat new age claim that existence is fractal, repetitive, and arranged into repeating, self triggering spirals.

THE PANTHEIST'S ARGUMENT

Within the context of pantheism, essentially that a great many, or possibly all deities, exist in some form, there is wiggle room for additional possibilities to exist- while monotheism presents only a limited number of possible arrangements depending on the nature of the deity in question, there are technically an infinite number of arrangements for the pantheist, in which there might be deities or forces from any number of the formerly listed categories- one deity, for example, might not punish anyone, while another does nothing but punish. For this purpose, Christianity serves as an example despite their insistence upon terming themselves monotheists- for Satan as they conceive of him, as an ever-living being (albeit one that will spend most of eternity suffering) is immortal and apparently capable of omnipresence, or at least being present in many locations at once or, as it may be, fielding armies of lesser beings doing the actual work for him.

Within Christianity, we have essentially four deities, and almost limitless demigods and other cosmic forces- we have Jehovah, a judge and executioner, said to be all powerful. There is, then, also, Jesus, an ascended messianic force, which almost opposes Jehovah, in that it is his will that all should join him in paradise- some Christian groups proclaim that Jesus has already won this battle and will, either immediately upon the death of the individual, or eventually in time, bring all life forms to his side.

Further, the religion contains a holy ghost- a sort of cosmic spirit which is omnipresent as it relates to human beings, and which might be said to be a sort of karmic, mystic potency, and finally we see the devil, or Satan, which is the equivalent of the "bad guy" god- a bit like a more confused Hades or Pluto, reigning over the unrighteous dead, but who will eventually be destroyed utterly and punished eternally.

Islam, too, contains elements of pantheism- Allah, Dajjal, Muhammad, Ali, various djinn of certain powers, desert spirits, and other forces, all of which have some combination of divine aspects, and most of which are said to be immortal- if immortality alone is the function of true divinity, then both the Christians and Islamists essentially preach that humans become gods upon death and judgment.

For the more self-proclaimed pantheists, such as Hellenists and so forth, it is surely possible for them to have beings which fall into various categories given- I know of no specific school of philosophy within Hellenistic religion that teaches that free will does not exist, and thus their variety of deities is more limited. While all Greek and Roman gods appear to have been anthropomorphic, some seem to have been more physical than others, such as Zeus often wooing human women in animal form, while I know of no tale from antiquity which speaks of a mortal physically encountering Hestia- Athena and Hermes, especially, seem to have often appeared physically to various warriors, leaders, and so forth.

If we have some combination of these different categories, then the equations become far more complicated- within a monotheistic framework, it is simple to categorize the different types of divinity which *can* exist, but within a polytheistic framework, it may not truly be possible to do so- the categorical order begins to break down as more parts are added, like a complicated machine that becomes unbalanced.

THE CHAOTIC OR EVEN PURPOSELESS COSMOS

The possibility of a purely chaotic, senseless, only temporarily ordered existence is one of the few other ways other than pantheism to ascribe any other characteristics to whatever force gave rise to existence itself. Within this chaotic framework, order is mostly temporary and/or illusory, and entropy, rather than order, is the norm.

I have, myself, studied materials from one group which preaches this specific doctrine- the Cult of Lilith, which regards order and even, to an extent, existence itself, as the perverted result of the prolapse of pure chaos in antiquity.

According to such teachings, a sort of gnostic-style non-duality of pure chaos is the pure state of the vast expanse which may be termed, loosely (for no true term man uses, I believe, can encompass the view perfectly) "everything-ness."

At some time in the long past, according to such groups, Jehovah, seen as a malevolent and selfish deity, discovered, through his own corrupt nature, that he had the ability to order this chaos, departing from a sort of Cthulhu-like primordial entity which rested in a cradle of pure disorder, with order relegated to temporarily formed and quickly destroyed "bubbles" which appeared in this chaotic soup, like holes in a block of swiss cheese.

In an attempt to maintain this supposedly degenerated "order" which Jehovah created, he enslaved everything that he created to physical laws, including his most nefarious works, such as sexual reproduction (for the chaos had been genderless) and concepts such as light and dark, rich and poor- or any other possible dichotomy used now by mankind to describe existence. The ultimate goal of this occult group, and apparently similar orders, is to return to chaos through mental self destruction, a sort of Lovecraft style attempt to go insane, venerating chaos, destruction, and everything ugly- the combined effort of such veneration, they teach, would be to split reality itself and destroy it, ripping the Christian god apart into everlasting torment.

In such a chaos-driven system (or lack of a true system thereof) order and logic begin to break down utterly; if such teachings are true, life is not only ultimately without purpose, but could even be seen as subjectively undesirable- this is vaguely similar to certain Gnostic teachings, with both good and evil, left and right, up and down seen as ultimately false terms, and a sense of being/nonbeing seen as higher than both. In these teachings, there are creative and destructive forces higher than existence, with the ultimate release seen as achieving such a state, where experience is no longer necessary.

In fact, ultimately, only if we regard the human experience of existence to be at least subjectively "real" or valid, does any logic applied to the divine realm become sensible. Even logic applied to the mundane, physical world, isn't truly logical, if the universe we observe is some sort of illusion or perversion of a more primordial, true order or disorder.

Even Buddhism contains, in a way, a similar aspect to these ideas- while the Buddhist system does not teach that primordial essence is a form of nonsensical chaos, it does teach that reality as we experience it is a sort of dream or illusion, and that things like logic and philosophy are technically subjective facets of a fallen existence which the individual strives to eventually defeat and exit. To the Buddhist, experiencing reality is a form of painful endeavor, which should be left behind in favor of nonexistence- it is a confusing concept for the western mind, and there are many inauthentic "Buddhists" in the west who prefer a sort of hippie lifestyle to the real mystic path.

The chaotic cosmos envisioned by some groups, where no sense makes sense (so to speak) would indicate that the physical existence we observe must of necessity be fallen and degenerate- since it organizes itself at least for vast expanses of time, and only (according to secular theory) after this enormous number of years, will it break down into entropy and collapse. This largely orderly existence seems to indicate that these individuals and groups are either in error, and wrong (and that disorder is not the norm, or even necessarily primordial) or that they are completely correct, and some sort of deity created order out of disorder with malevolent intent.

In a chaotic system such as this, it is possible for truly divine beings to have characteristics which might in the ordered sense be contradictory- a deity might possess infinite power and yet be utterly impotent at the same time, or occupy a physical body while being immaterial- a strange system indeed to the orderly mind of man- but this is the teaching which such groups adhere to. We might liken such utterances to the theory of quanta in science- a sort of material which at the same time is not truly physical, or may be neither or both- quantum theory seems to at least tenuously be in line with such chaotic theories, although further experimentation might change this fact.

CAN GOD LIE?

A more philosophical (rather than logical) concept is whether or not, particularly, any of these deities are worthy of worship- an all powerful being, surely, would have the capability to lie, and thus even the Christian god might actually be a lunatic of demonic proportions, delivering a message of salvation to the world with the singular aim of taking pleasure in gazing upon the recently deceased as he sends them, each and every one, to perdition and hellfire. If we presume an all powerful, or at least monumentally powerful, deity, then no characteristic, however contradictory of a particular religious dogma, can be characterized as "impossible" with regards to the deity, because the deity, like man, would be capable of vice, violence, spite, jealousy, and fits of nonsensical rage. Only by taking the deity at its supposed word, is this surpassed, without any evidence that the being in question is actually telling the truth.

The paradox behind this argument is as old as the sands of time- in essence, *can god create a rock so big that he cannot lift it?* Observing this paradox, it seems to defeat the very capability of an all powerful deity to exist. If the deity is able to create a rock of that mass, it is all powerful, however, it is simultaneously not all powerful, because the deity now lacks the capability of lifting the rock. Conversely, if the deity is not capable of making such a rock to begin with, his all powerful nature is equally destroyed.

We can apply similar logic to the topic of lying and ask essentially, *Is god capable of telling a lie?*

In some religious groups, the answer is an unequivocal "yes," and some malevolent beings may lie constantly, in attempts to fool or destroy other beings (usually human beings.) In some other groups, the answer is usually considered to be "no" although they never explain how an all powerful being can remain all powerful without having such a capability.

Within Christianity and Islam, the deity (specifically, the creator spirit) is capable of any feat- however, none of them wish to debate this point, of whether the all powerful nature of their god allows their god to tell a lie!

Normally, the excuse given is "god does not choose to lie" or "god can lie, but won't, because god is always good and loves us all." However, if the deity is capable of lying, it could be that their *entire religion is a trick designed specifically to vex the believer!* Further, in an even more openly heretical concept, the being *could intend only those who reject the given religion to achieve paradise, condemning all members of that deities' religion to torment!*

We could imagine, here, a bohemian deity that is all powerful or nearly so, and created existence with the sole goal of enjoying it, creating life forms that he, she, or it, intended to enjoy life much the same- sexuality, good food, music, and so forth- such a deity would consider, for example, those abstaining from such things as degenerate or "not fun" sort of like a child receiving a defective toy.

Such a deity, if we assume it is immortal and thus capable of long term goals which might stretch into the thousands of years, might itself design a religion, send down prophets, and so forth, proclaiming sexuality and music and things of that nature to be sins, promising to punish the sinners, while the true goal of the religion is to single out those who resist such teachings and reward them.

This revolutionary concept, I believe, has never actually been included in any philosophical or religious school either in antiquity or the modern age, although having discussed the issue with others, I am aware that others have thought of the concept before- it could be that no philosopher has ever dared to pen such words for fear of punishment, either of a divine or humanistic nature. The idea of an all powerful deity itself opens up all sorts of possibilities for the nature of the deity itself, because the deity may ultimately choose to lie about anything, destroy anything- we could envision here Jehovah going back on his promise of no longer flooding the world, and doing it over and over until every life form succumbs to a frozen and watery death. It is possible that this has been covered in some philosophical school or text which is simply not generally known to exist by the public (possibly because such views would be suppressed.)

This would even frighten most religious individuals should they discover logically that it is entirely possible for any truly divine being to stab their followers in the back in such a manner. Apologists normally point to biblical passages stating that their god is unable to (or unwilling to) lie, yet then ignore the fact that the bible itself, if the deity truly has limitless capabilities, could essentially be a book of utter lies.

Here we can also look to certain pagan groups and say with certainty, that not only did their gods lie at times, but could even be lied to or tricked- there is a famous story

in Greek religion about their manner of sacrificial ritual-
that the gods commanded that the people should slaughter
animals and create two piles of material from them, and
whichever the gods found more desirable would be theirs,
while that which was less desirable would belong to the
humans. To trick the deities, the people took the cuts of
good meat and covered them in the bones, and created a
second pile of organs, innards, and tendons- naturally, the
deities thought the pile of bones was less desirable, and so
humans were able to keep the good meat, sacrificing only
things which were not fit for consumption, or were less so.

Similarly, the gods of ancient times would lie to
humans on occasion, or at least mislead them- so too was
the case with the Oracles, such as the most famous, at
Delphi, who misled one nobleman to a great loss in battle
against the Persians- according to this tale, the particular
king was told by the Oracle that a great army would be
defeated, should he advance into Persia- he did so, lost, and
returned to the Oracle in a rage, asking her why she misled
him- he was then told that he failed to ask which of the
great armies would be the victor.

Only among certain modern, normally monotheistic,
and usually right hand path groups are deities regarded with
the type of moral and behavioral absolutism that contradicts
the stated omnipotence of these same deities- many divine
figures in antiquity were, if not actually mortal, capable of
human vice, pain, and so forth, such as Aries who would
fight in battle alongside any army he chose, fearlessly (for
he could not die) but would be wounded, and carry on for
days in moaning pain and agony. Apparently, other deities

found this annoying or humorous, and at some point he would be sealed in a jar full of medicine, after which he would recover, only to once again ride out to war.

DEITY ABHORRENCE, AND STEALING THE GODS

In addition to asking whether there is a sound basis for the worship of any particular deity regardless of its characteristics, there is a flip-side to comprehend- antitheism, or the abhorrence of a deity which is regarded as real (or the abhorrence of a deity considered not to be real, and hated on its philosophical or symbolic basis.)

In some practices and religions, we see divine figures which either allow themselves to be destroyed or harmed in some way for some higher purpose (Jesus supposedly allowing himself to be crucified, Odin hanging off of the Yggdrasil, or perhaps Shiva allowing Kali to trample him to quell her rage and prevent the world from being destroyed.) We also, sometimes, see the use of deities as spiritual punching bags of sorts, meant to be ritually condemned, spat upon, or rejected as part of some sort of ceremony, perhaps to curse its followers, or to stave off disease- a totem of sorts, which may symbolically represent sickness, and is then "defeated" by a ritual designed to shame or repulse this same figure.

The latter is more often symbolic in nature- for these beings are not mortal, and the ritual may not even be designed specifically to harm the being, but may be designed to pacify it- in some cases these religious or spiritual services are little understood.

Looking to the native spiritual movements of pre-Columbian Caribbean civilization (a topic I myself studied intently) we can see an element of this- totems, or physical figures of spiritual importance, representing various gods, would be held by the various tribes which may inhabit either a single island, or a part of an island- in such cases, the shaman (who was normally himself not superstitious or spiritual) would occupy a space below the figurine and manipulate it during rituals, such that the inanimate object was seen as animate by the tribe, who were almost always also on various hallucinogens which were used as sacraments.

If one tribe experienced famine, disease, or invasion, it may in such a case attempt to steal the totem of a neighboring or hostile tribe- the hope here was that by capturing the foreign deities' idol, any problems that were happening would cease; the colonists who first entered the island chains of the Caribbean and saw these things first hand recorded it as such. The other tribe, having lost its totem, would normally cease hostilities, fearful that their own deity would destroy them for allowing themselves to be tricked or beaten into losing their totem; it would then make reparations to the tribe which stole the totem unless they were capable of tricking the other tribe and stealing it back, and feasts and other rituals may have been held, in order to pacify both sides.

Similar rituals are seen even to this day in parts of

THE OCCULT NATURE OF GOLD

South America, where a tribe may attempt to steal or destroy the idols of their neighbors for various purposes- to extract wealth, gain the upper hand in diplomacy, or to break a curse supposedly set by the other tribe.

There are also examples of direct abhorrence of deities- we might see Satan in this same light as regarded by some Christian movements, especially those of a more superstitious nature such as pentecostal groups or snake handling cults.

Seeing that Satan is technically a judeochristian deity possessed of immortality and at the very least extreme levels of very physical ability, rituals designed to destroy, defeat, or thwart the devil can be seen as a form of ritualized abhorrence in these groups- of special note here, are both voodoo-infused and herbalist phenomena specifically ascribed to religious practices in and around Louisiana and other southern states, where the black population continues to practice rituals that have been used in their current form since the days of slavery, and in other but similar forms since ancient times in Africa- such as hanging certain vines (devil's shoestring) above the door of a home, or placing them under the doormat or some dirt in front of the door, to "trip" the devil, or any other evil spirit, upon its attempt to enter and cause mischief. In Africa, except where Christianity has spread, such rituals may still be used, although they are meant to prevent evil spirits, not Satan specifically, from causing harm.

FRACTAL EXISTENCE, INFINITE DIMENSIONS, AND OTHER ESCAPE POINTS

Another interesting possibility lies in theoretical physics in the form of the ten dimension theory, string theory, multiverse theory, and other, similar theories which posit either a limitless existence, or one which is far more complicated than the one understood by observing the physical realm around us.

Within the multiverse theory, for example, it is posited that the observable universe is just one of many (or an infinite) number of universes- that the plane of existence that exists within the third dimension of length, width, and depth, is infinite in size, and likely infinite in its content of material- such that even where space is empty, the amount of matter and energy approaches infinity- if the multidimensional theories are then applied, and more dimensions used, it seems that existence as we experience it during life only seems to have a real beginning or ending because of our limited ability to observe it- in such a system, were we able to see ourselves as we actually exist, we would see a continuous line in the fourth dimension which extends in either direction infinitely, from the time we are born, to the time our matter decays, and this would be intermixed with all other parts of existence, since the atoms composing our bodies came from other life forms or inanimate sources- there are associated theories, such as a sort of reincarnation which operates on a very similar principle, in which the line formed by our life bends back into some other existence, possibly vibrating randomly, ejecting our consciousness into a completely random life form as soon as death is experienced.

Any or all of these theories could be true- in which case the presence of a specifically judgmental deity likely governs only some sort of karmic power, which moderates the reincarnation cycle, and not much else. It is also possible that these theories could coincide with a deity which exerts a cosmic but not necessarily sentient force, a sort of innate or passive ordering of reality, which may also operate on these theorized upper dimensions as it may on the lower.

The fact that an atom supposedly operates on a similar basis to a solar system gives at least a sort of theoretical credence to such beliefs and theories- one may choose to think of an atom as a miniaturized solar system, perhaps populated by beings on a different dimension that are as unawares of our presence as we would be were our own solar system merely an atom, and our universe a single cell in an impossibly vast existence above ours, so large that what we consider empty vacuum is merely "less dense" matter on that upper level.

The western, linear mind often has as much difficulty comprehending the spiritual implications of such theories as a cycle-minded Hindu Brahman might have difficulty understanding calculus without any formal education in mathematics.

THE OCCULT NATURE OF GOLD

There are other possibilities as well, which at least share a similar type of philosophical basis- those who endorse a sort of pro-psychedelic, spiritualist lifestyle have, upon experimenting with certain substances, often reported astonishingly similar hypnotic visions of beings loosely termed "machine elves" which seem to them to hold sentience, encouraging the dazed nouveau-shaman to "create" a psychedelic reality through the use of sound, which may either be seen as a spiritual statement, or may be seen more as a psychological allegory for the story of deities which "sing" to create.

For these groups and individuals, the deity may be seen as the self- that a human being is a god in training, or that god is a metaphor for existence itself, or that the term "deity" may refer to some sort of energetic but not necessarily intelligible force that binds reality together, but has no further purpose.

In the principle of the fractal existence, we may sum up all mathematics as equating to *infinity* for example, and label finite mathematical principles and equations as degraded portions of this final equation. If proponents of such cosmic murmurings are right, then all things which can exist, must exist, in all possible forms, perhaps even in forms outside of our own laws of physics. In the fractal system, there would be gods, and there would not be gods, simultaneously, or perhaps separately depending on what existence you found yourself in.

Some are naturally predisposed to regard such theories as "hippie, new age nonsense" while claiming equally improbable-sounding material is true- and to such proponents, the idea of the finite and nihilistic existence of a deterministic atheist is as strange and awkward as those who claim an all powerful god that is yet finite in its abilities.

In fact (and as I will cover as well in this work) to no religion does any other religion, in a general sense, "make sense" because the principles of one religion, unless it is a forebear or offshoot of another, will necessarily be different, and to a substantial degree, or else the two groups would merge together, or diverge further from one another, just as groups within Christianity or Islam continue to diverge as we speak- the Shiites from the Sunni, the Pentecostals from the Unitarians, and so forth.

And this disagreement over the character of any deities which may exist has caused more struggle, death, and chaos, than any single, stand-alone philosophy has ever caused.

ARTIFICIAL REALITY: ANOTHER POSSIBILITY

One particular idea that has gained at least some momentum (and which, likely, all children who grew up after the 1970s have thought of at one time or another) is the idea that reality, as we perceive it, along with any deities it may contain, is a sort of artificial reality- a full-immersion style video game of sorts, in which the physical laws and structure of existence are concocted and not real-that at some point- perhaps upon physical death, or the fulfillment of some other goal, the "game" or artifice ends, and the individual, being, or other intelligence, emerges into the "real" reality. We might envision what we could consider an alien being strapped into a chair covered in wires and screens, immersed completely in the world around us- which is artificial in nature- essentially that each individual here is actually an avatar or character merely being controlled by the actual being.

However, this theory does fall apart somewhat on at least one logical basis- if it is true that we are merely avatars or characters within the vast, artificial framework of a sort of video game or alternate reality, one would think that the actual reality behind it, in which the "real us" exists, would be at least fairly similar and governed by marginally similar laws to ours, since the creators of such a reality would be limited by their own comprehension of the reality around them as well- for example, we cannot create, in our own realm, a video game which operates in the fourth dimension, nor would we be capable, likely, of understanding or enjoying it. If reality as we see it is artificial in nature, any purpose, from leisure to learning, could be given as to why it was constructed in the first place- and this hardly precludes the existence of deities- for perhaps we are ourselves deities immersing ourselves in artifice as a form of enjoyment, or perhaps the super-reality contains deities of similar types we discuss here in our world.

There is, interestingly, at least one experiment- the infamous double slit experiment- might, by some counts, illustrate a possible artificial reality- plenty of information is available regarding this experiment and its ramifications, but in short, it has been proposed that particles of light may act differently depending upon whether they are observed or not- in this case, light acts in both the nature of particles, and of waves, but seems only to act as a particle when observed (although it is not clear whether those interpreting the experiment in this manner ever replicated their results, so this may be a piece of folklore or fancy.)

IF TIME TRAVEL INTO THE FUTURE IS EVER MADE POSSIBLE, AND EXISTENCE IS ORDERLY, THEN DETERMINISM IS LIKELY CORRECT

There is one phenomenon that could resolve the issue of whether free will exists or not- it may not be possible to determine whether a deity or group of deities exists, or whether hellfire or some other judgment or punishment is administered to the dead, but on this point, science is not impotent.

If we imagine that in the future, a machine or method is developed which allows individuals to travel in time, and it is possible to move forwards (that is, into the future) then determinism must by definition be more likely to be true- free will would be an illusion, and existence likely came about from a singularity in which the movement of all particles and energy was predetermined and governed by absolute physical laws.

THE OCCULT NATURE OF GOLD

When I say, "more likely to be true" rather than "must, essentially, be true" I say so because the possibility of reality being an artificial reality, or a devolved form of primordial chaos, is still present- in such a case, time travel only precludes free will insofar as physical order is assumed to be absolute, but it would eliminate other possibilities, which assume that reality is what we are currently observing, as governed by an intelligent or cosmic force or being. If, however, time travel is ever developed, and it is determined that movement into the future is not possible, then it gives rise to two other possible scenarios, *at least insofar as we assume reality pertains to the observable.*

If it is found that movement into the past is possible, and upon moving into the past, it isn't possible to even return to what would be considered the "present" era (for example, a time traveler in 2300 travels to the 3rd century, and is then unable to return to 2300) then we can say that within the confines of observable reality, then determinism falls apart completely; free will not only exists, but the traveler has likely broken the continuum itself, and regressed all existence along with them- the new path of time will no longer be remotely the same. If we apply the butterfly affect within chaos theory (tiny variations cause drastic eventual effects to an outcome within a complex system) to this linear time, then by the time 2300 rolls around again, the world may have been destroyed by a nuclear war, or man might never have evolved past the medieval era and still be farming wheat and telling tales of witches.

If, however, movement back to the then-present era is possible, we might consider time an expanding and linear event- determinism thus is still more likely than before such an experiment, unless upon returning the traveler finds that his or her actions in the "past" have changed the present they return to. If 2300 is returned to, and things are exactly the same as they were when the traveler left (especially if they spent an extended time period interacting with the past, thus changing the course of existence) determinism can at least explain the phenomenon.

While only tenuously related to the topic of the nature of deities, this at least provides a possible future manner in which the topic of determinism, used in this text to limit all deities to eight categories, can be determined to be more or less likely than it is regarded presently.

DOES A TRUE DEITY REQUIRE OR EVEN DESIRE REVERENCE?

The most interesting topic of all, in my opinion, which can be discussed here, is simply whether a deity, which presumably possesses far greater power and ability than any human or other sentient being, would even desire or require reverence be shown to it. The question that regards us here, simply put, is whether a being which is all powerful, or nearly so, or which is able to create entire worlds, or destroy the universe with just the flick of a wrist, would even care what mere mortals think, believe, or how they behave.

THE OCCULT NATURE OF GOLD

The trend in most religious groups is to regard the deities as concerned with humans first and foremost, and almost everything else as an afterthought, sometimes designing all of existence solely to focus on our species of intellectually enhanced ape. From a philosophical perspective, it seems likely that more primitive humans, which developed most of the larger religions practiced today, simply did not know that existence was as vast as we know it to be presently, and that these older religions reflect this lapse in ability on their part. After all, if all of existence was relegated to the Earth, on which all existence centered, around which rotated various celestial bodies, with the stars as it seems "painted" on the sky which functioned like an enormous canvas, it would make sense to put humans, as the only "intelligent" species present, at the center of all divine or cosmic activity.

As the universe became larger, and man began to understand that his role in existence was anything but central, this changed- and even in antiquity, some celestially obsessed religious groups seem to have put man lower down than the larger religions practiced even today indicate as his proper role- the Mayans, with their calendars and observatories, seem to have seen mankind as little more than a bystander to cosmology, a species which the gods concerned themselves with only as slaves to supply them with blood sacrifices. In the modern era, now that we can understand that at the very least we occupy one functionally average planet around an average star in an average galaxy in a nondescript part of an expanding universe made up of insane numbers of other galaxies, new religious and spiritual groups have increasingly depicted man as, if not inconsequential, at least less important in an absolute sense- perhaps the bastard spawn of space aliens, or an experimental byproduct of genetic experimentation. Of course, secular groups lead the way in this endeavor, regarding man as an evolutionary product alone, without a deity to help him in his struggles, and when a deity is present, that deity is less concerned than those in the past.

Deism is the natural and possibly earliest offshoot of such beliefs- enlightenment era science gave rise to individuals who, shocked by their findings that space was more vast and man much smaller than before, nonetheless persisted in believing there was an intelligence behind creation. This watchmaker god set creation into motion, and apparently wandered off into the cosmos, bored with the universe, or at most entertained in a general sense, with what we call life emerging mostly by chance from a primordial pool of scum and chemicals, courtesy of Miller and Urey and abiogenesis; deism was born, and even many Christians felt that god was primarily interested in experimentation and observation, like a scientist who creates new life forms solely to see that he is capable of doing so.

This new, less interested being, either gave man free will and simply told him to play nicely with others, or else gave man no free will, and did not care what he did to begin with; and in either case, the god of the deist was less mystical and more "logical" than those practiced in the past.

INTER-RELIGIOUS STRUGGLE: WHAT "MAKES SENSE"?

As I stated before- the adherents (and especially leaders) of any particular religious or spiritual group, will invariably regard the teachings of dissimilar groups as strange, unorthodox, weird, and usually negative in nature. Only pantheists and new agers routinely regard other religious groups with any sort of applause, and even then, religious forces which break what they consider important moral or philosophical laws will be regarded as suspect.

The usual line of attack varies from group to group, but simply having some adherents chuckling sardonically about the strange beliefs of these foreign bodies normally convinces the other adherents of the group that the rituals, beliefs, or moral laws of the other groups' book or church are either humorous or dangerous- the media is often used as a cudgel by the reigning religious forces of a society to illustrate this purpose either in the form of yellow journalism or satire.

We can find no better illustration of this than to consider the first interactions between colonialists and the natives they encountered; how strange, to the colonialists, were the native rituals, worshiping trees and rocks and dancing about? How strange to the natives, were the colonialists, kneeling before a wooden cross and chanting to a corpse?

THE OCCULT NATURE OF GOLD

It is not my intent here to express any sort of cultural relativism- I view the very idea as a threat to the free world and believe all cultures should protect their traditions and rituals (so long as they do not unduly attack or harm those outside of the norm.) However, it is certain, that there would have been no difference between these two groups, and their expressions of confusion, when they first encountered one another's religions.

The nature of any deity is quite the same- an atheist finds it bizarre that anyone would choose to worship a being for which no solid evidence exists, a Christian finds it bizarre that anyone would worship a wooden idol carved from a block of sandstone, and a Wiccan finds the idea of a judgmental and invisible male deity to be quite funny.

To determine the nature of whatever divine force exists, is likely not even possible, given the limitations of observation as they relate to philosophy, and given the limits of philosophy as it relates to the topic of beings which may not exist, or may not be able to be proven exist. Here in this text, we are mainly considering the possible natures of deities, spirituality, and existence, rather than trying to narrow them further- which may be as far as man is able to go until he dies and finds out for himself whether there is a god, or goddess, or some sort of pantheon. Perhaps, even upon dying, man will still be left in the dark, possibly because there is no deity, and life is a purposeless and aberrant nihilism, or perhaps because he reincarnates forever, forgetting all past lives.

COULD GOD OR GODS BE EXTRA TERRESTRIALS? COULD WE?

The possibility that mankind is the product of some sort of extra terrestrial activity, rather than the direct result of a god, has caused fury in the last few decades, with proponents of these theories labeled heretics, pseudoscientists, and crackpots- however, most of their critics overlook the simple fact that the creation of humans by alien life, *doesn't preclude the existence of a deity.* In fact, not one category of deity I described is prevented from existing if this is the case, and it merely requires a new understanding of scriptural elements to even be compatible with faiths and paths which right now are openly hostile to this sort of material- a casual review of human history will find more human encounters with strange beings, sightings of UFOs, and so forth, than cases where humans have seen a deity, and with the latter, even some of these cases may equally be ascribed as encounters of more primitive mankind with some sort of more advanced sentient race.

If we presume that what man normally terms deities, are actually life forms from other worlds or even galaxies, then we can look at many religious scriptures and determine that they actually describe encounters with real beings, not with theoretical cosmic forces. Ancient religions seem quite explicit at times, in stating that mankind literally, physically interacted with their gods, seeming to regard anything with supernatural (or seemingly so) knowledge or abilities as divine.

THE OCCULT NATURE OF GOLD

The fact that the Christian god is based on that of Judaism, and that Judaism was henotheistic and seems to have copied Genesis from the Babylonians (who had altered Sumerian religion but retained its records) seems almost undeniable- the stories are essentially the same, from the world flood and the building of a boat or ark, to the garden of Eden, where either Adam (in Genesis) or Adamu (in Sumerian lore) was tricked (in Genesis) or gifted (in Sumerian lore) the fruit of knowledge, by a talking snake, which the Jews regard there as an actual creature, the Christians regard as the devil, and the Sumerians seemed to regard as an embodiment of a god called Enki.

Even the Jewish story of Lilith, which didn't find its way into the bible at Nicea, seems to have been based on similar tales of Lilitu from Sumeria- and here we're only speaking about Christianity, and ignoring the presence of, say, the Vimana in Vedic religion, or the sky people, star people, or people "from the heavens" which are found in tales which cover the entire world, from Mesoamerica, through Africa and Europe, Asia, and to the aboriginal Australians as well.

Often, such tales seem also to be linked with similar tales revolving around small pockets of mankind retreating into caves or tunnels to escape apocalyptic events above- most notably in Zoroastrian lore, where the benevolent Ahura Mazda tells the Cappadocians to build extensive networks of rooms and chambers below the ground, because of malevolent beings intent on destroying them- and many, many Mesoamerican myths involve mankind arising from the Earth, literally from caves, after an extended period spent below.

The possibility that what we regard as deities are physical beings seems more relevant when one considers the strange time line of human evolution, where after millions of years are spent developing an upright posture, expanded cranial capacity and increased neural convolution seem to arise in a time span more in line with artificial, rather than natural, selection, or perhaps even with genetic modification, along with "junk" DNA that appears, linguistically, to have been deliberately programmed.

Theists- those specifically that believe that any deity is cosmic and not corporeal- shun such tales, or else explain that any intelligence seen in the lineage of man's evolution or creation, appears so because of the intelligent design of a spiritual force.

All things equal, however, such a divine being could just as easily have created an alien race, millions of years before man existed- a race which, in turn, then created us in their image; and while ancient astronaut theories are condemned by mainstream science and religion alike, they nonetheless have a similar collection of at least theoretical evidence to assert their claims, as compared to the mainstream theist (perhaps more so) and perhaps are on par with secular science which claims human evolution was natural and uninterrupted by the interference of any intelligent force.

If such theories are true, then we might classify

these more advanced beings as a form of demigod- mortal (at least in theory) and limited in ability, but nonetheless more powerful and intelligent than our own species. In this case, both physical "gods" *and* some sort of cosmic creative force may exist at the same time, because the existence of one does not prevent the existence of the other.

The definition which we ascribe to deities or "gods" is another variable which perhaps should be considered here- if by deity we merely mean any being which is above man in terms of ability, then it's quite possible that such beings, in very real, physical form, exist right in our own physical realm. If, by gods or deities, we mean "beings not necessarily possessed of a spiritual presence, with supernatural powers" or "beings capable of creating matter" it becomes a different issue. In the abrahamist sense, a god needs to be all knowing, all powerful, and present everywhere at the same time, in which case any intelligent beings other than ourselves cannot be deities, and would be relegated to demigod or extra-human status at most.

The way in which a domesticated animal reacts to the flick of a lighter in the hand of a human might serve as a rough approximation of any encounter mankind has had, or is likely to have, with beings capable of traversing the cosmos in a timely fashion- a reaction of awe and perhaps reverence, which if these theories are true, explains at least some of the deities mankind has worshiped, obeyed, and sacrificed to.

THE LIMITS OF SECULAR SCIENCE AND ITS GOALS

Secular science, as it currently functions at the present time, has jeopardized itself and its usefulness on such philosophical issues, in part by becoming the dark reflection of what its movement towards secularity originally sought to avoid.

Originally, science was largely limited to the study of languages, history, and "chemistry" or alchemy, plus engineering, often applied to military matters or matters of government, by tribes or kingdoms capable of financing individuals who then would have been considered geniuses in comparison to the mostly illiterate population. These occultists (for what they did was considered supernatural and, when suppressed, was always veiled in stenography and symbolism) formed the bulk of innovation from the fall of Rome to roughly the renaissance, after which what we now term "modern" science began to revolutionize the world.

Originally, science was all but forced to regard deities as real, in part because anyone professing heretical beliefs was hung or burned, and in part because no philosophers, at the time, considered atheism to be particularly interesting or merited- science developed alongside folk medicine and superstition, with the most intelligent people in the average medieval kingdom being old spinsters skilled in herbalism who lived on the fringes of society, called witches by the laypeople, who nonetheless never failed to arrive at her doorstep when they were sick.

Now, science has gone from unconcerned with religion, to obsessed with opposing it- to the point where very intelligent individuals are pressured to publicly condemn religion; and in this I do not indicate that they should profess any specific religion, spirituality, or that choosing to condemn it is "bad" but rather that the educational system responsible for equipping scientists is failing them, in that science has gone from a system of debate, to a system of indoctrination- a situation which I must begrudgingly acknowledge, that the Christians are at least partially correct in their summations about, although they see it as an attack on the church, or on Jesus, rather than what it really is- a rule-based system in which opinions which are considered "too strange" are not just hushed up but suppressed actively through the peer review process.

Where once the great minds spent entire lifetimes debating the existence of deities, the nature of deities, the nature of reality, and associated topics, there is now a system in which free thought is destroyed in favor of memorization and fact-regurgitation, which makes for great engineers and terrible architects, and which favors boring rudimentary concepts over possibly revolutionary theories, which are expunged from the white halls and towers of every university as heresy, a modern day witch hunt, only with unpopular scientific theories standing in for the witch.

For the debate over the existence and nature of any deities which exist must naturally include individuals from all walks of life- and right now, the intellectual discourse regarding the topic is largely held between ministers and clergy of various religious groups, only rarely involving truly intelligent individuals capable of philosophical thought, let alone individuals capable of crafting their own theories.

APPLYING SOLIPSISM TO DEITIES

The principle of solipsism (in short *I can only know that myself truly exists*) may be applied to deities as well, forming a truly perplexing philosophical debate over any possible nature of divine forces which may exist.

If, truly, a person can only objectively know that they themselves truly exist, debate at first seems inconsequential- having established that even observable, physical beings around them might be illusions or extensions of their own mind, it would seem strange to then debate with these illusory other beings about the nature of even more beings which can't even be in most cases observed.

From a philosophical standpoint, though, the issue is at least interesting if not illuminating; perhaps the jealousy and sometimes pettiness ascribed to certain deities is itself a result of the deity being a solipsist- perhaps out in the cosmos there is a lunatic creator, which truly does not realize that sentient beings are actually sentient, considering us the way we might consider an ant, as a homogeneous, interchangeable, utterly expendable automaton. There might be an entire pantheon, of solipsist deities, who tolerate each other only due to their own immortal nature, and which themselves debate amongst one another over whether human beings can be objectively qualified as sentient, intelligent beings, or whether we ourselves are an illusion.

Although no religion seems to have considered this possibility, the fact that a solipsist deity or group of deities may exist is nonetheless present. A solipsist god would surely explain the suffering one may encounter in this world- from warfare to sickness, if we do not consider such phenomena as objectively bad or evil, but rather only subjectively so, from our own standpoint, then such a being may be entirely unconcerned with it, and may themselves be merely observing the universe as we might observe an aquarium, fixated not on helping the fish but merely watching them, and perhaps keeping them alive if only for entertainment.

We may at the same time consider an emotionally unstable but sane deity, also a solipsist, which may not be all powerful, and may be childlike, experiencing fits of rage in which the deity destroys living things, only to feel bad afterward and sulk for a time, pondering its own actions.

In fact, when an element of solipsism is introduced into any debate about the nature of an extant deity, it doesn't further limit possible natures, but allows for seemingly contradictory concepts and behaviors on the part of the god- such as a tendency to create, and then destroy, or to be all powerful, yet act at times as though it is not. This being, considering itself the only truly important, truly living thing in existence, doesn't necessarily have a need for logical consistency, because only its own whims and desires are important.

PERHAPS MAN HIMSELF IS GOD

And now, we consider the fact that, perhaps, god did not make man in his image, perhaps the reverse is true, and *man made god in his image.* This statement, normally made by atheists in an effort to confuse or anger religious individuals, is, however, worth consideration. This statement, in fact, can refer either to an atheistic sentiment and be sarcastic in nature, or can refer to the notion that mankind's collective consciousness is capable of manifesting such a being either in this world or in some other realm.

In the former case, man is truly his own master and god- for if man is the most advanced, and possibly the only introspective, life form in existence, then as the highest (subjectively speaking) life form, at the pinnacle of development, man should be worshiping himself and his own achievements, rather than an external entity- roughly speaking, this is the basis of Satanism, including the sarcasm, related to the ever-mocking black mass, or the adaptation of catholic litany to a Luciferian perspective and ritual system.

THE OCCULT NATURE OF GOLD

In the latter case, however, the statement refers to a more serious concept, which finds its place in certain occult schools and new age movements, that thought is able to direct, control, or in some way affect reality. If this is true, then it is quite possible that mankind's own belief in its various deities causes them to manifest- a similar notion to that of an *egregore* or *servitor* as discussed in some occult circles- in such concepts, naturally, the more individuals participating, the more (potentially) powerful the newly manifested entity becomes, so that a single person may create a sort of spiritual servant, while a culture may create its own pantheon of beings which begin to garner more and more power over time- this notion is somewhat limited, however, in explaining how dominant religious groups have succumbed to smaller ones, unless it figures the level of devotion and zeal into the equation and presumes that the smaller group was simply more devout, and their deity or pantheon thus stronger.

This loosely follows the concept of making dreams reality through action and obsession, such as we might consider the case with someone like Adolf Hitler who, obsessed with the idea that the Germanic people were a scattered remnant of the Atlantean population (or so it is said) proceeded to conquer neighboring states, either ordering or allowing various advisers, generals, and scientists, to scatter across Asia and Africa and bring back sacred texts and relics he believed possessed supernatural powers. We see this at work, also, with the Masons who founded the United States itself, who deviated from all traditional notions of the function of states, and essentially experimented as they went along, designing the nation in a way that was unlike any other, and even dissimilar from the French Revolutionaries, who nonetheless formed the backbone of the same idealistic system of individual liberty.

If it is indeed possible to alter reality (either physical or spiritual) through willpower alone, and through collective effort, one might say that almost any religion or occult movement is technically "correct" in its teachings, as long as its members display devotion to the cause- likewise, it would be the same for states, cultures, and even family units- an intriguing idea to say the least.

"Is God willing to prevent evil, but not able? Then he is not omnipotent.
Is he able, but not willing? Then he is malevolent.
Is he both able and willing? Then whence cometh evil?
Is he neither able nor willing? Then why call him God?" ~Epicurus

THE END

50551798R00035

Made in the USA
Columbia, SC
08 February 2019